CW00386416

Made Up Love Song

Made Up Love Song

Bettina von Zwehl

V&A Publishing

One of a limited edition of 800 copies

First published by V&A Publishing, 2014
Victoria and Albert Museum
South Kensington
London SW7 2RL
www.vandapublishing.com

Distributed in North America by Harry N. Abrams Inc., New York
© Victoria and Albert Museum, London

ISBN 978 1 85177 822 5

10 9 8 7 6 5 4 3 2 1
2018 2017 2016 2015 2014

A catalogue record for this book is available from the British Library.

Designer: Reena Kataria

All images by Bettina von Zwehl © Bettina von Zwehl
All other images photographed by V&A Photographic Studio
© Victoria and Albert Museum, London

Frontispiece: Bettina von Zwehl, *Made Up Love Song, part 34*, 2011.
C-type print (edition of 5), diameter 5.8 cm (frame 16.5 x 16.5 cm). V&A: E.76–2012
The print and frame specifications are identical for all of the works in the series.

Printed in China

V&A Publishing

Supporting the world's leading
museum of art and design,
the Victoria and Albert
Museum, London

Foreword

The Friends of the V&A are delighted to be able to provide the support for the publication of Bettina von Zwehl's new book *Made Up Love Song*. In 2011, the Friends of the V&A provided the support necessary for Bettina's six-month residency at the V&A. The images for *Made Up Love Song* were shot inside the V&A during this residency. Helping to enable the publication of *Made Up Love Song* is therefore a very rewarding and natural extension of the Friends of the V&A's support. The images are both haunting and atmospheric and quite literally capture the V&A in a new light; they bring a very human perspective to the daily life of this busy museum.

Introduction
David Chandler

As Neil MacGregor's book and BBC Radio 4 series *A History of the World in 100 Objects* (2012) has recently reminded us, the association of the profile portrait with ideas of power and dominion has a long and complex history that extends at least as far back as 300 BC, when Macedonian official Lysimachus used Alexander the Great's deified portrait on his coins to reinforce his position as Alexander's successor. Now, the surviving tradition of using such portraits on coins and stamps not only ensures the continuing currency of these ideas but reinforces the sense, too, that the profile is a form of distilled representation – the rendering of some emblematic essence of the person depicted; reductive, but also pure and strong, and, as in the mug shot, both accurate and unsentimental. But the significance of the profile, and its related form, the silhouette, in recording this essential, resilient truth about a person, has another, mythic history, one that trails back to Roman historian Pliny and a vignette in his *Natural History* (77–79 AD) about the origin of painting, in which a young woman, deeply in love with a man who is soon to depart on a long journey, traces in outline the shadow of his face thrown onto a wall behind him. Though there has been much philosophical speculation as to its meaning and legacy, Pliny's fable establishes another kind of enduring authority for the profile, introducing an explicit dialogue between the impulse to make a portrait and the articulation of love, one freighted with a particular sense of longing and imminent loss.

According to Victor I. Stoichiță, it was Swiss philosopher Jean-Jacques Rousseau, in his *Essai sur l'origin des langues* (1781), who first reimagined this myth of painting as one, primarily, of love: 'the first time that the outlined shadow was considered to be, not a primitive mode of pictorial expression, but a primitive language through which love expressed itself'.[1] Around the same time, Johann Caspar Lavater, the eighteenth-century physiognomist, saw in the outlined profile the mysteries of the human soul – it was 'a hieroglyph that had to be deciphered'.[2] But for the devout Lavater, as Stoichiță suggests, that very practice of deciphering was also 'an act of love, committed to searching out the divine in the human being'.[3] And perhaps the residue, for us, of these Enlightenment ideas, is our received understanding

John Miers, *Portrait of Isabella Burrell*, late 18th century. Paint on plaster. Portrait miniature bequeathed by Miss Grace Valentine Stephenson as part of the R.H. Stephenson Bequest. V&A: P.82–1929

that a portrait should be a kind of penetrating analysis, and, furthermore, that the most effective and enduring portraits are those that are the result of some connection, or even chemistry, having existed between the artist and sitter; some faint echo residing in the work perhaps of the original, mythic expression of love. Our awareness that these images are essentially illusory, representational fictions, does not entirely forestall that residual belief, and it might be said that the most interesting works of contemporary portraiture, especially in photographic art, are those that explore this tension between what might be revealed and what might remain hidden, between the visible and the invisible.

All these things seem to resonate with the photographic portraits of Bettina von Zwehl (b.1971), and in particular with the work she made in 2011 while in residence at the Victoria and Albert Museum, the centrepiece of which is the extraordinary, composite portrait comprising 34 images of Sophia Birikorang, titled *Made Up Love Song*.

Ideally, as with that enduring sense of the portrait's creation, the concept of an artist's residency in a museum is based on a form of exchange. For a museum of art and design, the presence of a working artist should reinforce the important and myriad connections between past and present on which its own work must be based. The artist's engagement with its collection will demonstrate, very tangibly, that the interpretation and understanding of art and its objects is an ongoing and ever-changing activity, evolving almost in the moment. Even more fundamentally, the artist's presence illuminates something implicit but too often taken for granted about museums: that not only are they the repositories of historic objects, but that they also represent and celebrate multiple acts of making over time. They tell the perennial stories of human endeavour and imagination.

As much as artists can invigorate the museum's spaces for learning, they too have an opportunity to inhabit a new space, and a new context for their own work. There is the potential for a new intimacy with a collection, of course, which may be inspiring, daunting or distracting in equal measure. But a sense of privileged access is also inherent to the building itself. Suddenly, its private as well as public spaces open up, the sense of its architecture changes, and

Hans Holbein, *Box in the form of a rose, with a miniature portrait of Anne of Cleves (1515-1557)*, c.1539. Turned ivory and painted (gum) miniature on vellum. Bequeathed by George Salting. V&A: P.153:1, 2–1910

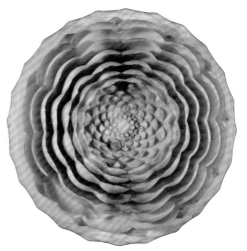

there are people, procedures and routines to negotiate – the atmospheres and culture of the institution to experience and engage with. One could see how all this could inhibit the creative process – what most artists crave, after all, is a protected space – but the temporary sense of belonging that a residency affords might also act as a catalyst for something new and unexpected to emerge, some new energy or idea to develop, and, out of this collective dialogue with the past, the artist can also take a step forward.

This was certainly the case for Bettina von Zwehl. Her V&A residency proved to be the perfect setting for her, and the experiences she had there – the ideas that developed and the work she made – marked a radical shift that continues to inform her practice. Indeed, from the outset, von Zwehl's principal aim was to develop new ways of working. Firstly, by building an extended portrait series with one sitter over the duration of the residency and, secondly, by considering making these portraits on a very small scale, to learn and deploy what she called 'the geometrical principles of the profile view', derived from coins, medals, painted miniatures and silhouettes in the museum's collection.[4]

Of these portrait forms, waiting to be discovered in the subdued light of gallery 90a, the painted miniatures proved to be the most important sources of inspiration for von Zwehl. In particular, she was drawn to Hans Holbein's picture of *Mrs Jane Small, formerly Mrs Pemberton* (*c*.1536), a work of characteristic economy and grace, whose striking realism speaks with great fluency across the nearly 500 years since it was painted, and mirrors closely the direct, simple elegance of the photographer's own previous portraits. In this remarkable image, Jane Small is presented, not in profile, but turned slightly to her left, her white cap and shawl and black dress set against a blue ground. Unusually among Holbein's miniatures, his subject is an ordinary woman, and the simple, even austere impression befits her status. But in this too, and in her features, Jane Small appears, uncannily, as a thoroughly modern woman; in repose, but also self-contained, without staged emotion or expression. Although Holbein scaled down his miniatures from preparatory drawings, the more common technique was to paint without preparation directly from life; the great immediacy and sense of revelation achieved by this method has often been compared to that achieved in early photography.[5]

Hans Holbein, *Mrs Jane Small, formerly Mrs Pemberton*, *c*.1536. Watercolour on vellum, stuck to a playing card with five of diamonds. Portrait miniature purchased with the assistance of the Art Fund, the Murray Bequest, and an anonymous donor. V&A: P.40&A–1935

ANNO ETATIS SVÆ 23

Miniatures were typically given as intimate gifts, and at their inception in the royal court of Tudor England, their bestowal by the monarchy expressed what Roy Strong once called 'the ultimate gesture of favour'.[6] Underpinning its courtly significance, the art of the miniature, or 'limning', was also associated with a sense of mystery – with secrets and technical tricks – and seen as a protected knowledge passed from one artist to another. To an extent, von Zwehl's work on the residency, referring directly back to that tradition, takes on something of its history.

The simple shift in scale in von Zwehl's work is important in itself. Over the last 30 years or so, our sense of the photographic object has altered considerably, with prints of a grand scale being closely associated with photography's increasing presence in international museums and galleries – a new kind of civic photography, we might say, that has also drawn heavily on the traditions and functions of painting. But while the expansive scale and attendant epic vistas or dizzying interiors of German artist Andreas Gursky, for example, revolve around a play with spectacle, propelling the viewer away from the pictures to take in the all-encompassing (and often illusory) experience of them – achieved by systematic digital manipulation and distortion – the scale of the miniature returns the photograph to its earliest incarnations. Information is condensed and refined into a density of detail that draws the viewer close, and reminds us that the history of the photographic object is bound up with holding, and with touch. As Geoffrey Batchen has said of daguerreotypes: 'we are made to behold the *thingness* of the visual – its thickness, the tooth of its grain – even as we simultaneously encounter the *visuality* of the tactile – its look, the piercing force of its perception.'[7] These remarks might also usefully apply to the miniature portraits that von Zwehl began making at the V&A in 2011; contemporary works that take the intimacy of personal exchange (and secrecy), and the minute, precious density of photographic transcription – with all its lingering sense of magical revelation – back into the public realm of the museum. Von Zwehl arrived at the V&A with a history of working in highly controlled studio settings. Her various portrait series since 1998 had involved making physical demands on her sitters – waking them from sleep, requiring them to exercise or hold their breath just before the portrait was taken – all strategies used, in part, to unsettle habitual human responses to the camera. For artist

Bettina von Zwehl, *Untitled III, No. 2*, 1998.

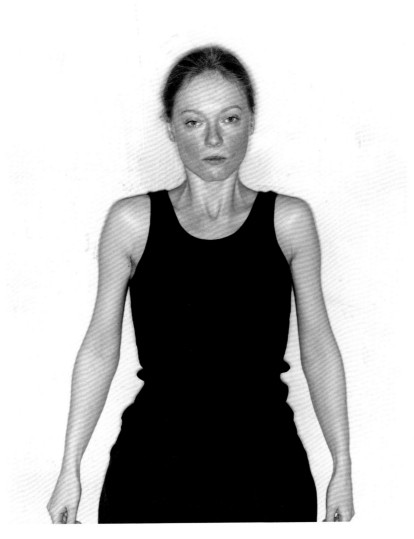

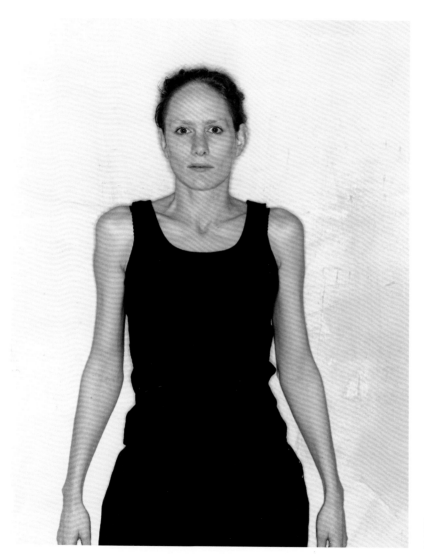

Bettina von Zwehl,
Untitled III, No. 5,
1998.

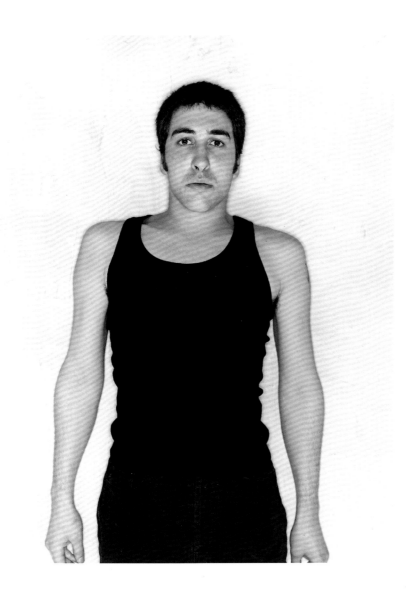

Bettina von Zwehl,
Untitled III, No. 6,
1998.

and sitter alike, the work was exacting as well as physically charged; the large-format, 10 x 8" field camera and flash system creating an intense, formal methodology that involved great discipline and co-ordination. However, the results, where the uncertain, distracted response of each sitter is balanced by a minimal background and the pristine fidelity of the recorded information, often belie these conditions – the image becoming a serene space where all the exertion of the living and breathing human subject finds a kind of composure and balance. If these series privileged description while calling into question the camera's capacity for psychological insight, von Zwehl's increasing interest in the portrait profile has intensified these descriptive priorities. They emphasize that sense of the serene space, in which, as in Holbein's miniature of Jane Small, the sitter falls into a kind of meditative reverie – not imposed on by the camera, not submitted for character analysis, but brought into the act of photographing as if into a restive place reserved for contemplation, for looking carefully and for thinking.

It was this notion of the profile that von Zwehl brought to the V&A, with the intention of extending it into a sustained project: working with one person over the duration of the residency. In her search for an appropriate subject, she began photographing various people in the museum, in the process establishing the potency of the new miniature format. But she eventually gravitated to working with the security staff, and particularly to the women. Sophia Birikorang was not one of those who stepped forward initially, but in her smile and shy reluctance there seemed to be a veiled level of interest and, after some further discussion and persuasion, Birikorang agreed to participate in the project, embarking on sessions which would go on, three times a week, for six months.

Sophia, a Londoner who came to the UK from Ghana as a child, had worked at the museum for six years. The portrait sessions took place during her working hours, usually in the morning before she started her shift, and, although she enjoyed the diversion, both she and von Zwehl recognized that they were both creatures of routine. Their meetings quickly established a comfortable pattern and a collaborative character. In one early session Sophia decided to remove her wig, a dramatic gesture that set the visual tone for their subsequent work as well as sealing the sense of growing intimacy between the two women.

According to Sophia, there was no 'putting on an act in the sessions, it was just "be yourself"'. The project also helped to revive her own artistic ambitions: 'I'd had an interest in photography but I'd lost interest in people until I met Bettina, now I'm going back to taking photographs of people.'[8]

The portrait sessions were conducted on the landing of the museum's great North Staircase, a site overlooked by a huge arched window, 6 metres high and 3 metres wide, originally containing stained glass panels designed by Reuben Townroe in 1864.[9] The stained glass was destroyed during World War II, but the current frosted glass has the advantage of bathing the landing area in a beautiful soft light, which immediately struck von Zwehl as she explored the building at the start of her residency. She had never worked with natural light before, but all her portraits of Sophia were made here, from week to week, under the subtle gradations of light produced by changing weather and the passing of the seasons, from winter to summer.

For von Zwehl the project introduced a less pressured, less rigid way of working; her meetings with Sophia generated a systematic layering of experiences that she likened more to the accumulative process of painting than to the conventional models of photographic practice. The routine was like a marking of time; it was slow and repetitive, but with each session offering and adding something new to the work. For Sophia, who had been reserved and reluctant at first, the portrait sessions helped her develop a new sense of self-confidence, and a more outgoing attitude at work, which many colleagues commented on; as she said wryly, 'the project brought out my creative side.'[10]

And what of the work itself? From over 40 portrait sessions, 400 photographs were made, and these were eventually edited down to 34. The circular format, with a head and shoulder profile looking to the left of the picture, is completely consistent throughout, and, to some degree, the deliberate sense of repetition here, and the act of looking and looking again that the work demands, mirrors and condenses the routine, cumulative nature of the pictures' making – and the course of a relationship building over time. The palette of the pictures is muted and consciously narrow; Sophia's clothes shift from grey to black against a dark background, and in doing so they add

John Watkins, *The North Staircase, leading to the picture galleries*, 1876–1881. Etching. Given by Mr G.C. Parris. V&A: E.820–1945

a little more distinction to the minor inflections of light rising and falling almost imperceptibly through the work. Soft light rests on Sophia's face and shoulders, delineating her features and lifting her profile from the background shadow to the left of the frame. The effect of this tonal subtlety, together with the fine-grain density of the miniature printed image, just slightly larger than von Zwehl's original medium-format negative, is an almost three-dimensional, sculptural concentration from image to image – echoing the relief surfaces of the coins and cameo silhouettes the artist found in the V&A's collection. Superficially the portraits feel identical, but a closer comparison reveals distinct differences in Sophia's posture and facial expression, which, in turn, suggest a sense of changing mood and atmosphere ebbing and flowing through the work and over time, through the days and weeks of its making.

For von Zwehl, the profile has become the most powerful way to represent a person. The half-view of the face suppresses our tendency to extrapolate some inner state of mind from external features and removes any implied sense of psychological interchange, either with the photographer or with the viewer, which so many portraits sentimentally exploit. The more detached profile study instead suggests an absence of affect; the sitter is not communicating, at least not overtly (the turning away from the camera is an act of separation, of withdrawal). An invitation to look, to scrutinize in an almost scientific way, replaces the distracting and distorting implications of an empathetic connection. But by extending the profile portrait of Sophia over 34 images, von Zwehl allows the minor fluctuations of body language and expression, so precisely and subtly documented in these pictures, back into our reading of the work and our sense of the person. These nuances do not dictate to us, they do not implore us, but working harder, more slowly, almost covertly, we may discover them through the layered moods and rhythms of the standardized format. What emerges over the entire span of the work is the beautiful unfurling of a complex identity, one breathing gently within the taut confines of the image as if called forth by it.

Made Up Love Song is set quite consciously by the artist at the centre of a number of intersecting histories. By means of her chosen style and means of production, and the delicate paring down of any information in the images that might disclose a sense of time and place, von Zwehl has created

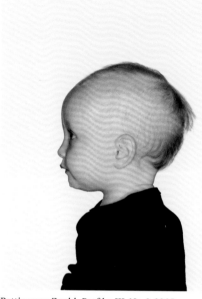

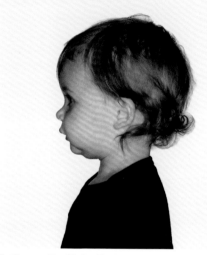

Bettina von Zwehl, *Profiles III, No. 3*, 2005.

Bettina von Zwehl, *Profiles III, No. 4*, 2005.

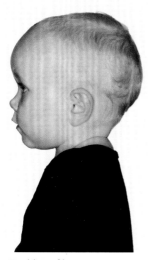

Bettina von Zwehl, *Profiles III, No. 5*, 2005.

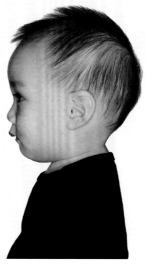

Bettina von Zwehl, *Profiles III, No. 6*, 2005.

a photographic form that appears to exist outside time. And here, in this indeterminate portrait space, the jewelled miniature's associations with the aristocracy and with the private economies of a social elite are intertwined with photography's nineteenth-century role in quasi-scientific modes of anthropological study.[11] The pictures of Sophia cast an arc over these social connections, one that evokes Britain's colonial past as well as its post-colonial present, and enfolds the V&A, too – its Victorian heritage, the history of its collections and the character of the museum now – in a complex narrative that leads us to think about race, representation and power. Over her 34-image work, von Zwehl's strategy is to conflate and amplify these echoes, but also to scramble them, to reform that history into a powerful contemporary statement.

Of course we know that this sense of timelessness is a sleight of hand, another act of concealment from among the miniaturist's secrets: Sophia's black 'necklace', for example, the only consistent motif in the portraits and a discrete allusion to her bejewelled forbears, is actually the plastic cord of her museum security pass. So for all its lack of specificity, and its international appeal, *Made Up Love Song* is fundamentally of a time and place. As much as the work is the creation of one artist it is also the product of a specific set of circumstances, at the centre of which is the opportunity, the space and time, provided by the V&A in offering the artist's residency. And in that sense too it is very much a London story, set in the here and now, in which a German woman and a woman originally from Ghana have come together, in a city of strangers where lives often intersect at random, to make something new and unique. In friendships there is much that can remain unsaid, and if for the institution this work might present itself as a fitting and useful emblem, the portraits will always enclose a more private and enigmatic exchange, and meaning; something at once more elusive and less malleable, an improvised and minimal love song made up of one repeated chord.

1 Victor I. Stoichiță, *A Short History of the Shadow* (London 1997), pp.153–4
2 Ibid, p.158
3 Ibid, p.160
4 Bettina von Zwehl, from her proposal for the V&A residency (2010)
5 See for example, Roy Strong, *The English Renaissance Miniature* (London 1983), p.9
6 Ibid
7 Geoffrey Batchen, 'Vernacular Photographies', in *Each Wild Idea* (Massachusetts 2001), p.61
8 From an interview with the author, 12 December 2013
9 For further information and illustrations of the original window, see John Physick, *The Victoria and Albert Museum: The history of its building* (London 1982), pp.88–90
10 From an interview with the author, 12 December 2013
11 For an introduction to this area of photographic history, see for example Elizabeth Edwards, *Raw Histories: photographs, anthropology and museums* (Oxford 2001)

Made Up Love Song

Sunday 11:00 am

Wednesday 11:30 am

Tuesday 10:30 am

Tuesday 11:30 am

Friday 11:00 am

Monday 9:25 am

Tuesday 9:40 am

Friday 9:40 am

Monday 9:25 am

Wednesday 11:30 am

Thursday 9:40 am

Thursday 9:40 am

Monday 9:25 am

Friday 9:40 am

Friday 9:25 am

Thursday 9:40 am

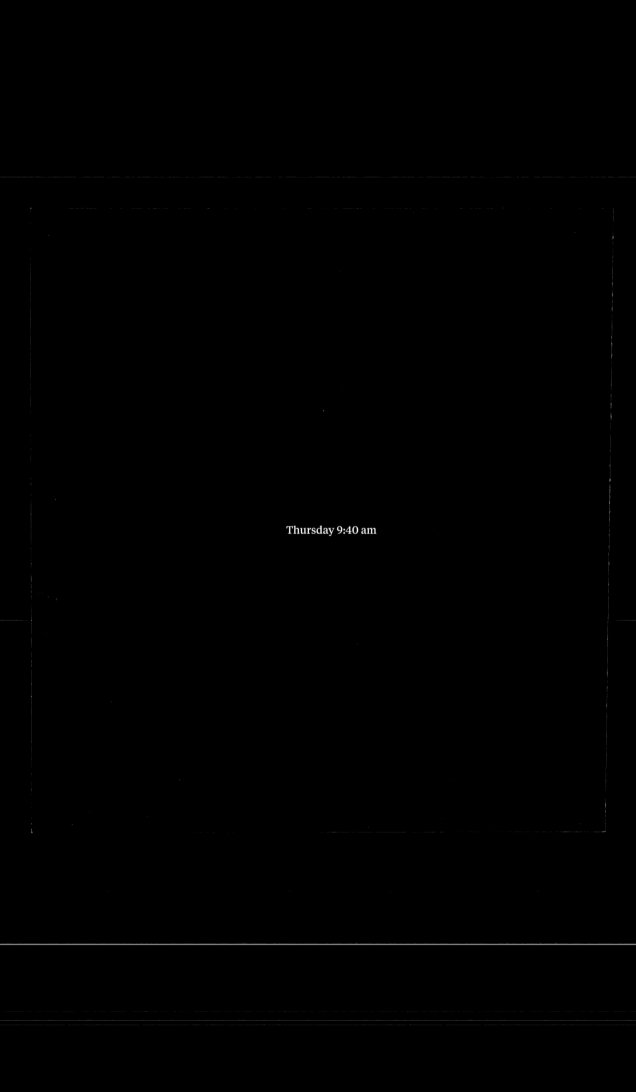

Thursday 9:40 am

Friday 12:00 pm

Tuesday 11:00 am

Thursday 9:40 am

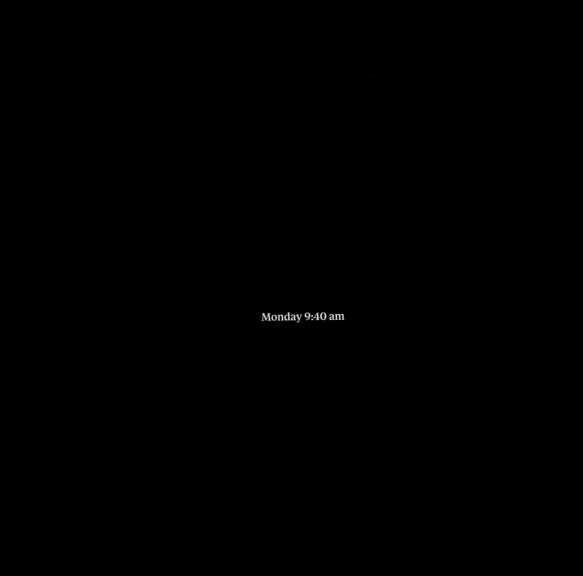

Monday 9:40 am

Tuesday 12:00 pm

Friday 9:40 am

Monday 10:00 am

Friday 10:00 am

Thursday 12:30 pm

Wednesday 10:00 am

Thursday 10:00 am

Monday 10:00 am

Tuesday 10:00 am

Monday 10:00 am

Tuesday 10:00 am

Monday 10:00 am

Wednesday 5:00 pm

Acknowledgements

My thanks go to Martin Barnes, Ruth Lloyd, Victoria Button, Chris Gingall and all the wonderful people at the V&A who supported my residency and the making of this book with their generosity, expertise and time. Special thanks go to the Friends of the V&A, V&A Visitor Services, Rebecca Hicks and Nicola Shane, Purdy Hicks Gallery, David Chandler, and David and Ruby.

I dedicate this book to Sophia Birikorang.

Biography

Bettina von Zwehl was born in Munich in 1971 and received an MA from the Royal College of Art (RCA), London, in 1999. She has built her international reputation on subtle yet captivating photographic portraits. Solo exhibitions of her work have been held at a number of leading European and American museums and galleries including the Freud Museum (London 2014), National Portrait Gallery (London 2012), Centrum Kultury Zamek (Poznan 2011), Victoria and Albert Museum of Childhood (London 2009), and Lombard Freid gallery (New York 2004).

Her photographs are held in the collections of the Solomon R. Guggenheim Museum, New York; Mint Museum, Charlotte, North Carolina; Victoria and Albert Museum, London; and the Rubell Family Collection, Miami, Florida. Bettina von Zwehl lives and works in London. She is represented by Purdy Hicks Gallery.